MW00747832

Shinto Poem Field
by
William Gough

144 Pages

ISBN: 978-1-927046449

A Gull Pond Book.
Design Consultant: Bronson Smith
Family Photo: "Dad & Me" ©1952

Shinto Poem Field

By

William Gough

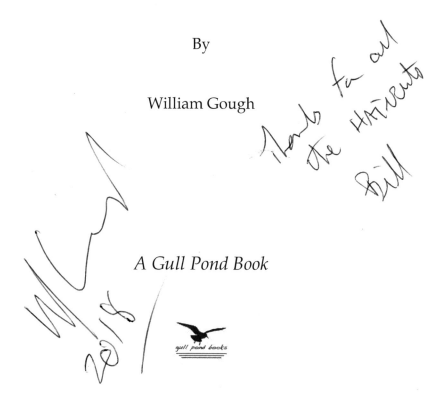

A Gull Pond Book

gull pond books

Table Of Contents:

Author's Note:

Since 2008 I've been tending what I call my *Shinto PoemField*. At one of my web pages, I publish poems in memory of friends and relatives who have died. If you want to follow the progress of my future gardening, please keep an eye on:

https://shinto-poem-field.yolasite.com/

At my age, I'm approaching the front lines, & it seems every month requires another poem. So, this book has become a gathering place for what I've already written – and I place them here in memory for as long as I may.

When it was time to design the cover, I came across an old snapshot of my dad & me. As I looked at the photo, it struck me – right in the heart and head - that this was to be the cover. In this snap, it's pretty clear that Dad was nursing a hangover & I was hindering his recovery – just by being a bratty kid. You can see the curled lip of a future poet.

I'd already been through a year in bed – my heart and life endangered, so I was no stranger to pain & possible death; I knew in my aching bones that I could die at any minute.

However, it never occurred to me that my father, Doctor Jim, would one day die. In 1984, I became painfully aware that he was mortal. His memory is threaded through these poems.

When you sit on your chair & wonder if you'll be remembered, take a moment to look around the yard, or check out the room. There may be a small boy or girl nearby. They could be spinning in a circle, screaming at the top of their lungs, & refusing to go away when your head is hurting.

Know this, if you have a little poet nearby, that kid is remembering everything; the smells, the sounds, the colors & the touch of flaking paint on old chairs. They'll remember the cadence of your voice, the way one eye stays open when you sleep, the days & night you're kind & they'll remember the days & nights when you're mean. Yet, somehow, in the alchemical cauldron of poetry, you will be truly represented; it all becomes right in a poem.

You may safely lie down at the end of life's long day & know that if such a poem-child glimpsed you even once, they'll wait, for decades if necessary, & then one magical month, they'll write & once again, your eager eyes will peer from the night; your feet will once again walk through daytime forests. A poet has caught a sighting of the most elusive of forest animals – a glimpse of you.

Prologue

Prologue

PHOTO ALBUM:

Something's happened
to my photo album.
It's filled with people
who lean on trees that
turn yellow.

Images set in picnic scenes
that tilt and curl
and buckle at the corners.

Like a snow storm
gummed corners
fall and blow around
the figure of my father
smiling through a glue-on
mustache
smiling at me.

As I close the album
I hear,
from inside,
the folding of tablecloths,
the paper
falling of the picnic dishes.

I walk down the street
and see the wind
blow fingers crooked,
bend knees,
and chill the bone.

In one lone room
I see the proper lover
(from days
when he could lift a sepia house)
pose,
lifting the girls at
a faded picnic.

The man who had the snapshot muscles
lies caught upon his bed.

He could spend all
night bathing
his hands in heated pearls,
&

the wind would spin around
his wrists.

Still
it would feel
like they'd
hung a stranger's
hands upon his arms.

His room is yellow
&
its corners curl.

FRIENDS OF MINE

At this time of year I find myself thinking of my maternal grandparents' best friends - the Gills. I'm back in the Newfoundland of the early Sixties, where I'd head through snow or rain to their home to deliver Christmas Gifts. Little did I know that the future would blow memory winds towards me every time I felt the delight of arriving at Merrymeeting Road in St. John's, clouds of breath settling on and freezing to snow-speckled paper.

Meet Mr. Gill.

He has a book of Plato in one hand, and is doing a Charles Atlas dynamic tension exercise. A genuine teacher, a modest man, a scholar and good friend to my Grandparents and myself.

THE FIVE PHILOSOPHY LESSONS
OF ALEXANDER STUART GILL

Lesson One:

In his corner grocery store
Alexander Stuart Gill carefully reads
paperback editions of Plato,
never cracking the spine.
Eventually he returns them
to the distributor, unbroken.
His eyes grow distant
he doesn't hear anything his wife
calls out to him.

As lean and snapped together
as a clasp knife
he buckles and clicks in my memory,
smiling and lifting
cartons of potato chips.

Lesson Two:

I became aware of him first
when I saw him do a monkey dance
at a time when I was short enough
to be beneath the clouds of cigar smoke
eyes to eyes as he buckled

with his back straight; a fur hat on
inside the house - a lit cigar in his mouth
arms folded like St. John ambulance slings.

See! He kicks his feet into the world.
"See him, come see him! Stu can do
the monkey dance!" calls Mrs. Gill.
"Don't split your pants!" screams Mrs. Case.

He sits on a fulcrum
of air and laughter.

Though they are the best of friends
my grandparents laugh at him, because,
as they say, he reads philosophy every day.
"I don't know what that word means," I say.
"No one does" my grandfather brays in laughter.
I become aware, a child who cares
what others think. Not yet knowing
how to use, as bandages, ink, (a child easily hurt)
I see, that no matter what they may say
Mr. Gill does not give a shit.
He doesn't care a bit; no matter what,
he laughs & does the monkey dance.
The cigar burns. The smoke rises.
Again, "Stu! Don't split your pants."

Lesson Three:

Memory placed in approaching Fall.

He now carries one paperback
all his own, does Alexander Stuart Gill.
All summer at the cabin of my grandparents
he reads his one book over and over again.
The same book. "Look out, Stu, you'll hurt
your brain." I now read a book a day
and when they run out of books for me
I forget what I read and go to cereal boxes
until new books are found. I hang around
the grown ups until they drop their magazines
and pick them up to read. I am a small boy
who is a word-thresher.
I sit behind a stack
of books and magazines,
leaning elbows on my knees.
I am so young
that I do not need glasses.

Alexander Stuart Gill reads the same book
again and again and again. I hesitate to ask
him about philosophy. Too shy to ask I try to see
if, in what he does, I may learn this philosophy.

He drops his one and only book
pushes and locks
his hands together,
his arms spread, a sturdy grip.

He pushes and pulls his hands each one against
the other. He yells "Dynamic tension!"
"Charles Atlas!"

My grandmother hoots, My grandfather
chants and sings, "Ninety pound weakling"
"Save it for the comics," laughs Mrs. Gill.

Mr. Gill yells:
"Self with self. Self against the self!"

When he finishes dynamic tension he runs
outside into the rain, a 1958 man
& does his monkey dance.

It is Fall. And I still don't know:
what is philosophy?

Lesson Four:

When Fall and Winter leave
and early Summer nears
and Spring housecleaning
catches up
with the cabin,
and mice run into the woods
and whiskey jays eat old crumbs,
Mr. Gill takes me to the forest,
past the mice, out of dust
and past the toadstools.

Near a tree in shadows
are more shadows.
"That's where they live, the little
People," he says.
"There, Billy, near the moss, and
because they are not fools, they'll welcome
you if you will welcome them.
Without words
they'll understand you,
and when they see the 'you'
I bring to see them,
they'll twinkle like lights
in the night of an outdoor Christmas tree.

And he is right.

Lesson Five:

It's bright summer at the cabin
of my grandparents;
the logs are fresh
painted and Mr. Gill
is outdoors doing
his dynamic tension.

Face down on gray
faded boards is his spine-cracked paperback.
He stops and looks at me, waiting.

The sun wheels overhead & skids
to a stop at noon.
Our shadows are dots at our feet.
"You're all exclamation points!" says Mr. Gill.

The sun rolls again and shadows stretch towards
the water from our feet. From somewhere my father
shows up with a Kodak home movie camera;
"Do something," he shouts, "anything!"

Mr. Gill," I ask, who is Plato?
And what
is philosophy? What did he say?"

"I don't have sound," shouts my father,
"This goddamed thing does not have sound.
Don't talk, for Christ's sake do!
Do something, anything!"

My father, when he speaks, roars.

My sister runs to the lake,
puts a toe in the water
& stops, frozen at the shore,
but smiles and waves
the kind of waves people make
in the fifties for home movie cameras.

My grandmother and mother are in
the kitchen and so do nothing for the camera,
though they do provide smoke to roll
around my father.

My grandfather peels off his undershirt
& also smiles
at the camera, flexing old muscles,
Dipping cold water from the well
he points to the white
circle of a dot painted, still fresh
upon the well's lid; white against the red.

Somehow in all this there's silence.
And, in the silence, Mr. Gill tells me
of a cave of shadows; of a fire with shadows
that crawl upon and over the wall.

He says we're between the shadow and the fire,
& somehow as the smoke from the kitchen swirls
around us, I'm in the cave where Mr. Gill
tells me that philosophy takes us
through the shadows,
helps us climb
into a chariot,
and whistle at four horses
who leap and lift and take us through the shadows
clinging to the edge of the chariot
& when smoke clears,
for years and years we see
people - we learn to see & learn
to feel not what is shadow but,
(he touches
me upon the arm;
his hands strong from dynamic tension)

Instead of seeing shadows,
we learn to see what is real.

Then he stops speaking &
simply points
a finger at the sun.

And I look through the sun.

I hear the whir of the home movie camera
and the words and world begin to whir.

I am dizzy in this whir of all there is
and all the voices and what I can see
is what I used to call the lake.

It holds what I used to call
reflections of the trees.
I am small
but I can see.

The sun clinks a glass against a cloud.
The Little People, I believe, are sleeping.

My grandfather gives me a drink
of water that is in a metal dipper.

When I drink the sun flashes in the water
into my eyes and I blink.

The water is cool
as cool as the shadow of the world.

And Alexander Stuart Gill
does a monkey dance
round and round the collected works
of Plato.

Remembering Gary R. Snyder.

Just because friends leave - vanish into that realm of death, it doesn't mean we forget them. O, Gary we still speak of you daily & are thankful for the friendship.

Here's the poem written for Gary's Memorial Service & for our friend, his wife, Teal Maedel.

Friends remain united, no matter if the earth is in or out of shadow.

TIME FLOWS – FOR GARY & TEAL & US ALL

One:

Time flows over the landscape
Time flows over us
Time flows
Time.

A Plane is flying
          So high that there are no countries.

A Plane is flying
          So low, it, aluminum-sail-fish, glides the ocean.

Teal leans against the window
over the ocean – seeking a sighting of Boston.
Lights flicker – at three in the morning
wingtip lights reflect themselves
sliding over the tide.

Teal sees her reflection in the window
Looking for a man she's yet to meet –
seems like lives ago – that time.

On that day of the flight
on that day of the arrival

Gary Snyder – walking to the Charles River
past the Hancock building – remembers how it
shed its glass skin
Lights blinked ::   falling sheets of glass
trembled – bent, became spherical.
A round rainbow hit the Charles and bounced:
a rainbow burned into the clouds.
"One wish" said Teal to the rainbow
as it bounced across the country
"One wish" said Gary to the clouds;
to the rainbow in the center
of each cloud.

"Teal Maedel" says Gary
– sounding out a new name.

"Gary Snyder" says Teal
– sounding out a new name.

This, all before we all gather.

Teal adjusts the time
on her watch &
Gary has left the river,
is nearly at the three-am airport;
They turn through darkness –
a common center drawing them to each other.

When we watch meteor showers
(say, as an example
burned across and
into our eyes) the *Perseids*
we seek the
radiant ;
that point which grows and throws meteors.

That point.

The Radiant
becomes a point formed by the meeting
of Teal and Gary
meteors ripple from that point.

Radiance.

Time beats ;
Time pulses ;
Time flows over a new landscape.

Two:

Paintings, brushes, pens,
coffee cups, rivers of letters
river walks – Boston meeting

Vancouver waiting;
before Bellingham.

When Teal and Gary meet
their childhoods meet
& in shadows one child finds another.
And in light; hands (now linked)
children run to a new Forest to play.
Escaping into the day.

Thru time their stories unite

Crack –

Teal hits the ball
& runs
while Caren waves her on.

Crack -

At Fenway Park, Gary is on his feet
a home run clears the wall & he heads to Kenmore
square. He gathers Rob and Scott to him,
and he and his kids
walk through the night.

Teal rounds third base, heading to home.

Home forms.

A circle turns –
they dance, they fly,
they join together all who must be joined.

Hands giving
touching, painting,
hands pointing at eagles
wheeling.

They know, as know we all,
all time is circles.
Events, like August meteors,
burn through their moments
The night sky holds illuminated lines,
the sky whirls itself,
so we know - the planet pulses,
light goes on, life ends,
life starts, life concludes
life flows over time
&
time is stilled.

They reach towards each other.
Months fall like burning flankers
from Gary and Teal.

Time
ticking

a meteor flames
the sky flings flame.
The circle grows, and we circle in this circle
all of us looking at each other.

Glasses raised,
Glasses lowered.

The look in their eyes
as they see each other
connects in such a way
we see their eye-beams
blink like plane lights
& they dance together.

Children in grown-up coats;
feet on sand at Savary.

Eagles spinning, diving, grabbing, lifting.

Eagles laughing at morning.

Claws hooked
two Eagles pinwheel past Mount Maxwell ;
they turn like clock hands
tick – tick – ticking
and two children
dance.

Three:

9-1-1.

As Gary waits to fly to Teal
as Teal waits for Gary,
one plane holds Gary as buildings melt &
fall into New York Streets;
three planes leave Boston – two crash
one flies high, higher
climbing, climbing.

While Teal waits to see
if Gary has made it through
the firestorm to their marriage,
his plane climbs above,
far away – to safety.

But she can't help thinking "What if"
And as they gather us together
to dance & drink & eat & laugh -
to whirl together in their time
– we
raise our glasses
see them joined.

We're meteors in an August sky.

Paddles dip – drumbeats calling the stroke,
the dip, the ripples,
as the Wedding Canoe
approaches Gary's boat –
paddles in the water
drumbeats
hearts drum
& Teal and Gary leap over the broom
&
into
their new lives in life together.

Two meteors light the Perseidian sky.

Blink.

Blink.

Four:

August brings meteor showers
and this early gathering.
By the time of this "now",
the Radiant has shaken meteors
across the sky;
new nieces – stars rolling into day
a granddaughter – eyes twin beams
of light.

And Teal and Gary have appeared and reappeared
to all ;
have found their way with kindness in our homes
and hearts
and gifts are left everywhere
they go.

Late night laughing
early morning music
all day exploring
feathers, fog, sun, day, night
they travel the world to see each other
again and again new explorers -
children.

"Night Teal"
"Night Gary"

We've had enough of illness.

Brave sons,
brave partner -
for brave Gary
has a journey.

Bright yellow meteors
explode sixty miles up
and Gary leaves us in a storm of meteors.

I think
the true hero is the Perseus who does not slice.
the true hero is the one who looks Medusa
in the face & knows the truth
& shares it as he drops his shield
looks death in the face :
that kind of hero.

Our true Mother is the Earth
our true Father is the sky;
lit by flames and bathed in water
directions flow from people
and together we are North, South, East, West
together we become Gary
and hold memories
like children hold their paper lanterns
at night in Beacon Park.

We walk together and hold each lantern
and light spills on the ground, into sky, and on our faces.
And in the light
we see his face
turn slowly,
blink
look our way
meteors fly in a night-time sky.

Time flows over the landscape

Time flows over us

Time flows

time.

*When I was a teenager I doubted that I'd ever meet a brother
and a sister who liked their parents. And then, one day I
visited Adrian Fowler & his sister Rosalie. As soon as I
walked into that house on Fleming street, I knew that I'd found
siblings who liked their parents. Not only that – so did I.*

*Stan Fowler reached his hands out for a two-handed
handshake, and Madeline Fowler beamed to meet me. I sat
dazed and had a cup of tea. And still I'm dazed.*

*Little did they know that when a teenager walked in to
Fleming Street, a poet walked out with memories tucked into
his backpack. They're gone, and I unpack this poem.*

FRIENDS:

Whirley
gig,
the god of time,
has spun Stan Fowler
like a windmill at the sun.
And each face that he leaves
to box the compass
is as definite
as a Wimbledon Morning.

When the wind stops,
and every bough breaks,
Stan tumbles
down
into an early morning
tennis court
where the summer heat
melts ice cream
on his long gray flannels
and Madeleine, his wife,
laughs
and tells him not
to mind,

"After all, Stan, it's
only ice cream."

The sky holds more
than clouds
it holds the soul
of Madeleine.

Somewhere between the blue
of summer time,
and the spun glass fog that spins
the light around the harbor,
her soul is drifting
and all the tea
time talk,
the streets,
the green of a fresh painted
fence gate,
fades for her.

Our moves unravel
like
an old sweater.

Somewhere
round a corner
she hears an echo
of a day when,
as a little girl,
she ran
and felt
the tickle to her knees
of a July field
that reached halfway
to the sky.

Now,
happy as a daisy,
Madeleine
catches in her throat
the green.

"Look,
see the way
the sky is folding me.
Oh,
if you could see
the way the sky
is flying like a swallow.
Its shadow flits
along the sea."

The wind has stopped

and Stan is walking
in his garden.
This year the flowers were
early,
and snow has covered tulips
in a flour bag.
Stan walks towards them,
and crouches,
waiting for the sun.

Ian McDonald was one of the smartest people I'd met, and he loved philosophy. I was young enough then to imagine that we'd be having a constantly-evolving conversation about Strawson. One that would evolve over the years with friendship; change as my mind changed.

And then, one day, as sudden as a sentence, I heard he was dead. He was one of my first friends to die, & as I drank steaming tea at the funeral home, I found things to say to other friends. It seemed profound at the time, the words echoed what philosophers had to say, and yet.. I felt empty, sad to the marrow of my bones.

And then, another day, this poem arrived, & somehow, I knew that what needed to be said was just fine in a few words – words of my own.

I'd learned how I could say goodbye to my friend.

THE LONG WALKER

The long walker
has caught my friend.

For Ian he chilled the bottle
with his hands
and warmed the malt with his breath
until, in a hospital bed,
the walker slipped his index finger
nail
inside the skin
and pricked
the peritoneum.

Then
all the thoughts
of Spinoza
the chuckles
over Strawson
the puzzles
over
Socrates
lay with marzipan head
a candy
in
a
casket

while we sipped
tea
in nearby rooms.

He touched our lives, we said,
So quick,
another
dead.

Then
snow
held our footsteps.

Spring has come
and dead Ian
is breathing
blossoms.

Bill Herskovic.

I'd only met him a few times at the home of his daughter & her husband. I was friends with Max & Mich Keller and loved going there for bar-b-ques – for Family Seders, or just to drop by.

Every time I went, I'd hope that Mich's dad would be there – true, he always had interesting things to say, but even more than that – it was the way he said "hello."

He saw me – in the middle of my Valley years – & that was unusual - to be seen in Los Angeles.

BALANCING BILL HERSKOVIC:

The first time I saw
Bill Herskovic I knew
he was a man of balance.

From all the wounds he had received
he'd become a man who reached out to others;
and there he was,
his hand moving towards me
a strong and easy handshake.
I was a stranger to
his family – early days of a complex
and yet easy friendship.
I saw his hand, as if in slo-mo,
reach forward and grip
and welcome me to his family.

His eyes, his touch, his laugh,
a quick grip of a knowing hand upon my shoulder,
as if adjusting
me and my face to hold more light,
to bring the features from the shadows.
I've followed magic far
too long not to recognize another practitioner.

His eyes joined his words,
"Bill - good name - you are welcome."

Where others had said, a long time
ago, to this man,
"You - your wife - your family are not wanted,"
he now reached ahead, & followed his handshake,
to ensure a stranger would feel wanted.

He tilted his head, looked at me
- and I mean looked
deep and clear and nodded,
as if in one quick glance he'd seen
who had entered his family's room,
and the things in me that needed balance.

The room felt warm, the floor grew soft
and the light that is in every human being - increased.
I knew that in the room, and outside the walls;
down the hills of Los Angeles,
and beyond - past ocean, land mass,
and in the smallest town
all had, somehow, become his family.

His reaching out traveled far into the world,
His camera eyes had click-clicked,
held the images of
all he'd seen

– his focus was unusual
enough so when I drove away,
the traffic seemed brighter,
oncoming lights made me squint –
a sure sign that I'd met a man of balance.

When I heard years later,
that the warrior of peace
had
left the building we call the earth,
I felt a sudden absence
as if a familiar spirit had gone to his reward.

Weeks passed –
the space filled in;
the day became what days become
– his absence had left what he'd abhorred - a lack of
balance.

I knew he'd left, through all his gifts,
another 'ring-off' tone
that would survive him far beyond his going.

And yet I felt this lack of balance.

He'd hung on through the deaths of those he loved,
the births of those
he loved, the strangers'
faces who needed his silent gifts,
the care he took with
family.
He could have lived,
I thought, even longer – so connected
to the world, the way light
is filtered in Los Angeles,
grandchildren's faces,
his family gathered
at one of their famous welcoming meals
 – where strangers become
also, for their time in there – his family.

He'd nod and watch, and despite all he'd seen,
take time to see again and listen.
He remained quiet - often to the side
of things watching. I'd see what he was doing
as he sought connection, would move forward
after a time aside
 – a word here, a touch there,
& the room would be
rebalanced.
I wondered why he'd used this time to leave.

For me, the writer, it always takes
a long time
to write – the death of others
hits me in the heart
in a place where I can't say a 'something';
many times, even an 'anything' is far beyond me.

I had to leave my work
to find the time
to follow
my true work.
That's the way I need the space of time;
It takes a while.

The pen may be a powerful tool,
but it is slower than a camera,
must draw from the world the light, pull
lines across the page;
coax tints and shades and shadows many times
until that light is placed just so
– the words reflecting light.

Bill Herskovic would know what I mean.
The sentences need to weight
the right amount,
the lines connect to each other

– the light that is in
each human must reflect
& echo in the page.

That kind of work.

This morning, in my own time of rebalance,
I awoke, and saw in my
mind's deep eye – two things:
the absent section of a well-lit room;
a missing friend I'd hardly met,
who left an imprint on the silver-salted-plate
that would not fade.

And on the other side, where we dwell for a while
on this place we call Earth
– a simple e-mail from his daughter;
"Nicole and Seth had a baby boy
this afternoon at Cedars Sinai Hospital.
4 pounds 11 ounces and 18 inches long.
Nicole and the baby
are doing well
and we are so grateful for the miracle
of life bestowed
on the family.
Will send email pixs soon. "

The light increased – and I could see quite clearly
that the time of leaving had been chosen
with the knowledge that
as one person left
another needed to arrive.

The room grew still.

The floor leveled off
(that sense after
an aftershock
that the earth has
settled again -
a simple moment)

an offering from a departing
man of balance.

Martin Lavut ...

was a gifted director, and he was also such fun to work with.
The two things do go together.
His mind didn't settle for easy answers. He'd a sense of joy,
oddity, and a keen perception of the hidden sorrows of life. That
makes for a key seat at the best table in the big Casino of film-
making.
Martin and I worked together a lot – it was a delight being a
producer when he was director.
This poem was finished after it gripped my heart and mind
during an overnight flight to Newfoundland.
As I wrote this poem, I knew I'd leapt, feet first, off the edge of
an eternal cliff & back into film and video. He continues to
inspire even after his death.

Goodbye Martin. You are missed.

http://www.theglobeandmail.com/arts/film/martin-
lavut-eccentric-filmmaker-made-people-open-
up/article28920775/

DIRECTOR'S CUT:
THE FLIGHT OF MARTIN LAVUT

1:
Places Please:

Somehow, I'm flying thru a sky
I've not seen till this year,
      &
for the first time since my wartime birth
that sky is one
where Martin Lavut's gone missing.

It took a full month's flight of thought
before his death entered what's left of my mind
the world, until now, had kept
me believing that Martin
might be still alive
but
his death took till today
 to leap into my thoughts
      &
cast him centre screen
falling, leveling off,
flying low to the ground,
director's lens to his eye, blue coat flying,
Mickey Mouse on a chain

behind him,
made of black and white piano keys
melting
into Mickey's WTF eyes,
and
wind-whistling mouth.

I'm aboard Flight 1134
heading towards Montreal.

Martin's sliding beneath the plane
Just under the left wing
We're over mountains,
 dream-diving
          &
Bursts thru the Rockies
light streaming thru
his own eyes/ twin-eyes-photon-beams/
night begins to sprocket in
24 frames a second
and I see his vision on a cloud,

Our audience
(called the passenger list)
thinks they're on a flight from Vancouver
to Montreal...
well...
I know we're all in Martin's movie
          &

for the first time
since he died
I get to cry as,
before the scene's described,
Tears leak down my cheeks
to smear the window,
while darkness moves in to hide the screen.

I wait to hear his wondrous & wondering
'Action'
        &
I cry quietly in my window seat...
while 'places please' echoes
in my mind as my seat-mates
shift – ever so slightly –
away from me.

They had the good sense to bring their own food
to the Airbus,
a sensible thing to do,
        &
they continue to
show sensibility in the way,
without a word,
they continue to lean
away from me, and do Sudoku while
I scrawl this poem-movie upon a page,
draw breath again,
then grab a tablet

&
hook movies
into a virtual rug
across
my iPad;
slam crooked fingers
against a virtual keyboard.

You know, weaving while slamming down
the pattern of this
word-movie.

I am
the kind of seat companion
you hope won't sit beside you.

Yeah, me.

Leaning ahead, and sobbing quietly (I hope)
as Martin flies beside the plane,
I know he's back again...same as before
leaping into
at
&
through movies...
...he looks
as startled to see me
as I am to see
he's

just as much alive
as light and shadow.

He climbs upon the wing
like Dante crossed with Rod Serling
and says
so only I may hear...

Places
please.

2: Lights...

Oh, oh, the spotlight hits me
and makes my
seat-mates
squirm, and shade their eyes.

They look around;
no empty seats upon the
eternal flight.

I feel like telling them
don't worry
I'll always be leaving.

The worst thing about being a nomad
is that I slide in and out of lives I love;
always the one to say good-bye;
to fly on different flights,

to leave forever
day or night
day for night
night for day
always sliding away
a sort of Scarlet Pimpernel
masked by nomadic cognition.

Clik/

fill-light streams out of
Montreal 1983.
source- home for
Martin,
and all Old Montreal
had been waiting for him...
as we made another war film together,
I can see that year embedded in the moon
when we made another movie.

3: Camera:

This
is what we live for
writers/producers.
directors/grips/camera operators
props/make up /costumes/
people who love old cars/
extras who want to look

like they've been time traveling/
a minute on screen
a night of shooting, months
of prep
we spend to dream this dream just right
enough so home TVs and screens
can suddenly shudder
and stream the banks
of virtual
rivers
splash in and out
of 1983
disguised as the 40's

4: Action:

Cars are rolled along the street, suddenly active;
actors smoke and walk and talk
        &
jump out of the path of cars
that are propelled by guys pushing
hidden in the lee side of each shot
        &
all through the streets
there is the sight
of us
dreaming with our eyes
wide open
as, like a bizarro Disneyland
 leader,

Martin jokes and laughs
(Mesmer with a megaphone)
        &
We think that we look
moderate & sensible
(tho neither of us is moderate and sensible
for we were hit on the head as children
by movie reels that
fell from the sky)

Sure,
we talk and make decisions...
but then
the scene takes us,
so perfect that in each
second of the shooting we fly above the world
we've all built
while it holds for 10 seconds, 20... more...
the car rolls out of an alley
and extras jump
        &
for one moment the screen is us.

I think how magical it is
to live our dreams
nothing said, till he, in
rapture, almost forgets to cry 'cut',

but does.

A spectator asks...
"all night for one minute?"
we hear this as if a Martian
with an accordion
has landed
in a field-hockey competition.

Film-makers make
 Bureaucrats go Crazy.

5: Cut:

"Once again!"

While waiting
he tells me of his memory-movie

that plays across his inner screen
when he's
back home making pictures.

He and his dad
had been in a restaurant
in pre-enlightened Montreal,
his ears had swiveled when he was a little boy
he, who overheard everything,
was with his father
and from a fifties table

he heard some Anglos
throw words like darts…

...I thought...

        they allowed
        none of them…

...in here...

Martin and his dad see the upturned sniffers,
the
brows
that raise independent of the other

        ...Jesus, next thing you know
        they'll say something in Yiddish
        or in French...

The Anglos clear the table
of themselves without
paying.

Years later
This version of a "them"
(a Newfie and a Jew)
roll worlds down
the ten pin alley
that we call film

and wait to hear
it's a wrap

and so it seems it is...

The end holds
and does not fade...

......for a month
now
it's been burning titles
into my mind
the end
the river
in a whirlpool
near
a bend of time.

Every detail of scant moments
burns in my mind
lit by images on nitro-infused celluloid
&
my nose
Bassets
towards
that sweet smell when a silent film
canister is opened.

Not currently producing..

I'm between lives, ready to slip,
as 70 clicked by, back into film
again.

When Martin shows up
flying beside my airplane,
waving at me, showing me where
I'm to stand
so I may remember
how he did it
and
take into the river
what I learned from watching him;
it's like a rerun of my favorite films.

This is a no-brainer

like Georges Surat's picnic
or
inner pointillism
or
an expanding screen of chloroform
or
the way a room becomes a sparkler
when I'm on tequila
each dot detaching from another dot
        &
I see Martin as I last saw him...

when he says...
...yr in a plane
so
why not jump
without
a
parachute?

One minute I was working on
another poem
about Hollywood Gargoyles
            &
when
I looked out the
window as we lurched into
Montreal
thru clouds,
            O
it was Martin once again;
not a cloud that looked like him,
but the
deflected beams of light that enter water,
refracted light...
...light sent out from the dreaming mind
and back again...
in short,
cinematically real.

Martin Lavut zooms beside the plane

to dendrite the movie of his life
        &
permeate my mind
molecules that
with stick legs,
roll endorphin boulders
towards receptors:
Time is a big boulder.

I carry Martin's poem with me when
wheels touch down
in Montreal
        &
Mind-clouds
tint in red edged memory
photon-painting Martin in my mind
and
if I write non stop...
weep a little ...
...let my mind
see his face slide into a metal-nailed puzzle
or
push thru a
screen of plasticine smells
he'll become
again
Claymation-real.

Martin and the head of Mickey Mouse

run down the aisle....
       &
it's time for me to say,
how much I loved working with you
my friend,
tho I went missing
        O
I left Toronto
simply because of being
the elusive Bill Gough;
always gone before he's found.

In any town, I'm the one who's recently left
or arrived
who thrives on being the vanished one
as if that's how I breathe
in
        &
out
the beginning
       &
the end
so I ask myself what
I will do to remember Martin
and decide to rebirth myself with joy
       &
direct as if I were a boy
just leaving Charlie Reid's ReKay
theatre that

started life as a chicken coop
 and turned into
the movie of Norris Point
          O
we sneaked our smokes in Norris Point
while Martin was sneaking into the
movie
of his dreams.

Instead of simply walking
Into the Montreal airport,
I fly myself into the air, and leave behind
the memories of my other
lives
vanishing
like a dream almost recalled.

6: Opening Nite:

Martin you
have left behind a mantle
of
courage
and all I need
do
is drape my shoulder,
when a nebula spins stars to make
 a cape of light.

I will zoom over St. John's with

director's eyepiece;
lens held in a squinting eye
 like Otto Preminger gripping a monocle,
falling back
to earth to quiver
over Rawlins Cross,
hit Cabot Tower,
deflect and bounce
to George street
where
drinkers glacé at the pinball
with attached
megaphone
and ask
    ...who the hell
    just fell
    from the sky,
and look,
behind rolling cameras up to a cloud
where Martin is still
directing
catching the image of
me hitting.

7: The Rerun:

Time drifts away
and time-winds
play a jig
for massed spoons

                    O
time is a crazy dancer ...
who still says 'o yes...'
even when our bodies drop
and wrinkle
and fall around our ankles
like Marilyn Monroe's bathrobe
on a rainy winter's nite.

I leap into these few
remaining years
no longer afraid

just frayed
beyond a daytime daydream
          &
during the decades that I've
been falling
teeth yellow,
 and go missing,
 flaps
bend where there was once a surface/
milk being poured
in slo mo
to
this time
when I am wrinkled and have
forgotten
my name

I will, for a moment before,
think of how Martin might record
this final scene... and call us all
to *places please*
and set the lights
the cameras
the action,
for that final grim dissolve...

          ...NO...

...sez my friend,
remember that our bodies are simply
megaphones...
and the second
I do
I'm standing by the old Hub
the 24 spokes are spinning
and as I shout
'places please'
          Martin looks over from
          our first film together,
          &
waves a last
good bye,
 his pendant
hanging from
one cloud lit by the full moon
of an orange sky

that paints Signal Hill,
spills down towards the Narrows,
and washes
till I cannot see the sky.

What I now know is
that even
when he's gone,
Martin is still
saying
places please...
lights...
camera...
action...

and all the rest is up
to us.

Places
please.

Roll Credits
for
in this case
credit
is
always
due
to the man who looks towards us

for
his
Close up
&
Dissolve to:

Martin Lavut: 1934-2016

RELATIVE DEATHS

Mom...

*I wrote this poem for my Mother's 93rd birthday. Finished it
the morning of her birthday, and printed it out at Chancellor
Park, where she was in the arms of long-term care.*
*It was a day of parties, and flowers arriving from people who
also loved her.*
*And at the end of the day, I joined her at her table and got to
read the poem directly to her, while watched by two wonderful
residents, the Devine Sisters of singing fame.*
*We all leaned around my reading of the poem. The habit in
Newfoundland was for listeners to punctuate a poem with
comments and smiles or frown, so the poem is, in many ways
breathed in and out in a room, until the true matrix is that of
all our breaths into a room of echoes.*
*The next time I read this poem aloud was after mom's death. I
read it when I spoke at the funeral. As I read, I could feel the
breath of that last room, where I read her a poem, in the
rhythm of the way her friends rolled along the halls, or tapped
with walkers.*
This Birthday poem turns out to be mom's Memorial poem.

*Now, a link to a page that talks just a bit about my mother,
Ruby (Case) Gough.*

http://www.newfoundlandpress.ca/

MOM AT 93:

Somehow, as mom turns ninety-three
and I slide towards seventy one,
it's time to write a poem
about what glorious fun
it is to simply sit and talk
while days dissolve and, in
memory, hold faces from the past
as clouds slide along the
last trace of light-lifting sky
where Cabot Tower spins a top;
a hub of empty spokes of "why?"

"Why" drifts away, as water goes past
every bend in life's rough steam,
dives over and past its falls,
over-flows the banks of youth,
takes us a-tumble into years of truth,
far past the shoals of "should"
and into still, deep pools of "could."

What I most love is the way that mom
always knew how to ask the necessary questions,
of... how I was, who I had become... and how,
for my Sister and for me, she could
(O, such a simple word) assist.

Instead of penny-pinching to the grave,
she, like Nan Gough, reached in
her apron pocket, and simply gave.

And so, for mother and for son
the sun rolls down the south-side hills,
spilling years before it, like a bolder
creating pebbles; spraying in the hop from
slope to slope, until the rock splashes down
into darkness of inevitable seas.

The Atlantic enfolds and holds us all
in salty arms; the lives that light the
spiralled sun, our eventual roll into
a deep peace that only subterranean
caves can give, the treasure chest of
memory of each life lived.

'Tis Peace that gives us peace, no
need to preach nor speculate on lives
lived like ours, with odd barnacles
of encrusted poverty rasping off
the liberating luxury of all things
& settle down to a precious few details;
the chair rolled to a window, a simple touch,
the shared hours that mean so much more
than 'must' or 'can.'
In short, we're already here, in St. John's
(Ireland just across the watery street)

ready to meet anything we may have to meet.

Sunset carries in its jaws
the husk of years and decades too,
when knowledge falls apart;
this is not so much the story of a mother and her son
but rather the simple feeling of each heart-beat,
the nodding at the sky,
the sounds of wheelchairs in the halls,
the residue of lives as down they run
and splash back to that Signal-Hill sky.

We're all related in this place;
have left the land of "special,"
of all the things we should have done,
that history of the bored, where
the ultimate shroud proves to be
but a tut-tut-tuttering.

My family true, the frontliners, move
in shades of red & green & blue, and ask
of our mother, just what they may do to help.
I walk by her room, and hear, "Ruby! We love you!"

I see the bathroom ritual, where they wrestle
gravity and laugh with mom,
while, down the length of
Ruby Road, I hear without fail,

the whispering sounds made
by the skirt of Florence Nightingale.

Talk is always cheap they say, but not the
murmured question, the turning of a husk at night,
the pillow moved just so; the right feel of
the bedspread near a curling hand.

Past the shallow pomp of what we own,
far from the cruise ships of the almost-rich,
a necessary gathering takes place where
we are, all of us, meeting beside a well
that we've often dreamed to life.

Know that when we spin towards those
final waterfalls, the hidden pool, we'll vortex
until we bend our pretzeled selves
into a bobbing fetus again, for,
floating in our mother's womb,
there are no cars, no money-men nor awards;
instead, a plain hammered dipper
is dipping into the well
that we've all used in our dream.

Some day, I'll see mom walk towards the well,
and I'll see her mother, Nan,
reach towards her and extend a simple helping hand.

One day, I'll take my turn and stepping nearer

as does she, & walking towards the circle on the red,
while all humanity draws near,
we'll pull the forest
around us like a needed screen...
...a simple life in Delphic style
where the great truth of life is revealed
by the eager way my mother rolls along the hall
or gains sweet enjoyment from the go-bus to the mall.

When all is said and done,
my mother's truth is such a simple one,
that we, all over the globe,
are ready to hold
each other's hand
as we approach that final well.

A breathing-in, and last-breath-out, so easy
to do, that we may now relax, smile, play the saw;
eat a bit of cake, wonder if the snow may
go tomorrow, have a dance or two, visit
Tim's one more time.
Relax, as what is the most clear note
of the bell-like sound when dipper hits the well-wall,
means that each second is eternal,
and we are, in infinity,
made mortal once again,
are mobius-stripped to
an infinite now.

Drink deep well water, brothers
and sisters of the clay;
and my cousins all,
make no fuss, for we
know, without doubt,
there is no terrible journey ahead of us.

Know that the place we most want to be
is
here
right
now
beside
the well
where
we stand together
close and yet forever free
as time shakes the
world,
until, at last
we realize
that
our own true mother
is turning
ninety
three.

Nan Gough comes to mind in times of sadness & she comes to mind in times of joy.

Many of my first memories are of her – and of her husband Newman. If you've read my book-length poem, "Ocean Of Childhood" [http://stores.lulu.com/williamgough] you've already met them as they arrived. Now, it's the time to write of them after they've departed.

As I set down the words, I want to highlight and delete the news of their going; to somehow reach through the pixels on my screen, & watch them re-form on the keyboard; to play a game of growl with them, to share a coffee, to simply sit in the same room as my grandparents - at the same time; to have them back.

I miss them.

NAN:

The seed has silver handles
and at its center
my grandmother
is a kernel
of sweet meat.
From the front pew
we weep at this mahogany
suffering;
the husk
the deep brown
red
the sheer size of it.
Words spill down
the aisle
rolling near our feet
resting warm and woolly
round my grandfather's ankles
soaking up his tears
thoughts of my grandmother
shove me around
in a long-forgotten
wooden wheelbarrow
that rattles and tips at every bump
and I feel the wood beneath
my three-year old hands
as all the world is long grass
that tickles my fingers

and at the last tip
my grandmother
Nanny Gough
lifts me in the air
&
spins me around
to hold me close
&
looks at me
&
smiles
a smile
so warm
that in my mind
a seed is cracking.

LOCKS:

My grandmother
is haunting
her old house.

They say
she opens doors that are locked
as tight as iron bands could clasp a barrel.

No matter how keen the lock
no matter how thick the deadbolt
when people leave a room
and my grandmother's ghost is
loose
locks fling apart
doors throw themselves wide open to
the room
when
any person would expect a door to
stay locked
for
ever
and perhaps
a day or two.

In day time when ghosts are
supposed to be still
she isn't.

With one hand braiding her hair,
the other,
almost as an afterthought,
is reaching into a door to pick the lock.

Her hair is still jet black
the color of a fine solid hair dye.

When people wondered why in the world she wouldn't,
while still alive,
let her hair grow white ("gracefully")
she found, did Alice Stead,
the blackest hair dye in the world
& made her braids gleam
like a fresh-polished stove top.

So strong was the dye that
it's lasted well into death,
locking color on her braids.

Now, in her old house,
she is flicking locks apart
and spinning cylinders past Orion.

They say she opens all closed doors.

You may ask if I,
who loved her so much,
and who now knows of a house
where I may reach her spirit,
plan to go there?
I'll have to answer no.

I, who felt my heart crack open
in her smile,
say
there's no need
to see her ghost
unless
she's learned some new tricks
since she died, for when alive
there never was a door,
no matter how locked and dead-bolted,
to any heart
she could not open.

When I was hurt by
words,
when I had locked my heart
against all grownups,
she would sit beside me
and casually braid her hair,

and, just as casually,
unlock my heart.

That's a better trick
than any ghost, even if she is my grandmother,
could do with any door.

Newman John Gough – in my mind I walk down into the
basement of your house. You look up from the workbench,
pliers in hand, next to the coded mason jars, where every screw
and nail was filed away, just the way you wanted.

Somehow, you're fading.

The body gone, the trace is like an early Instamatic blip-flash-
flaring at a birthday party. My eyes water, & there is an
image that slowly, slowly melts before the room comes back.

THE MAN WHO WEARS HIS JACKET IN ALL WEATHER

The man
who wears
his jacket
in all weather
is looking at the sun,
he feels the wind's fingers
touch his hair.

He lets the garden's
lilacs
brush sweet
against his face.

He squints even when
the cloud
chills
down the light
and never feels
the cool go across
his forehead.

The path around his
house
is made of
cockleshells,
and, when he walks,
the crunch
reminds him of a broken cup.

Inside the sun porch
his wife is sitting
surrounded by the scent
of Noxzema facial cream
and holds a
lace handkerchief
against her lower jaw.

Their house is small
but has some rooms
that neither ever
uses.

Behind the house
the mountains wait
to hold the sun.
Inside the house
the sunlight is dappled
and warm.

Both old,
they know enough
to spend
their days in silence.
And all that cracks
the quiet,
is the crunch of cockleshells
and
their creaking rockers,
mixed with
the ticking
of
the kitchen clock.

William Freeman Case.

He's now gone from us, the cop & warden who loved freedom.
All his training, his lectures (later developed for the teen-age
version of me) his endless opinions vanished as he realized,
when I was seven, that I was old enough to drive a car.

In my memory I am always driving & know his hands have
left the wheel, & somewhere round a skidding corner his big
laugh echoes to see how I can handle each skid on life's gravel
road – the place where nothing, ever, is really paved.

We all drive big cars on loose roadbeds.

SMALL HANDS ON A BIG WHEEL

My grandfather Will Case
his thick hands upon the steering wheel,
sees Deer Park's dirt road
chewed up by winter & then by spring;
rattled by cow catchers
dusted & then sprinkled
by water from Father Duffy's Well.

The water has spread a mantle.
The mantle is still as a bird
listening to a feather flutter
to land with other
fluttering feathers on the road.

I am seven and sitting on my grandfather's
lap & see in the rear-view-mirror
the bald sunburned head of
my Uncle Jack Case
as he lunges to the floor
of a '52 Dodge.

I am sitting on the lap of my grandfather.
my grandfather is younger than I now am
& in that now of then,
my seven-year-old hands
rest on the rest of the steering wheel
playing at driving
just below his hands
on the steering wheel.

The road is still until my grandfather laughs
& Uncle Jack Case groans
because he knows my grandfather will leave
my hands alone upon the rim of the wheel
which grows round as barrel hoops
when the speedometer needle
sticks and we stick lazy as dust to the road.

I feel the wheel rattle
and hear Uncle Jack's heart beat
"My God, Will, the child will kill us.
We'll be killed by the child!"

And so you will, Uncle Jack Case,
but not by this child who is driving in 1952
- not by seven-year-old Billy –

instead you'll die by his simply being
driven through the years
with your own speedometer winding
past fifteen years
&
my Uncle Jack Case does die
thrown by his bursting heart into the sky.

And when I pass the age of twenty-eight I see
my grandfather's hands buckle
& he cannot smoke without
someone giving him hell
for smoking & so he sinks into a pillow
like smoke is sucked into lungs downwards
downwards as
I get older
& pass him a cigarette.

He draws in and sucks the smoke
until the curls of smoke tickle his lungs.

We smoke together.

'Who gives a shit?' I ask.

He smiles & lights one smoke with another.

Curling into a bed,
rising through the hospital roof,
exhaled like thin gray smoke into the morning.

My father
fell through his own lungs
when I hit thirty-nine.

And I can clearly see in the rear-view mirror
all the dying & the killing - the way
the world spins parents deep into her arms
all this is easily seen in mirrors.

Not only death
is passed by the still-speeding car,
so is life passed.

My head turning as I drive thru life
I go faster, faster until my own children
fall from me
bouncing from the seat and out the window
bouncing into life
their own hands small
ready to grip
the wheel
as they bounce into their own cars.

I give them driving pointers,
but they're all too fast for me.

My hands, it seems are large
upon the same wheel
as when my hands were small :
my ringlets
are thinner now
&
I feel the breeze upon
the top of my head - how strange
strange indeed this breeze blowing hair away
sucking, I swear, the color out of it - see
the red go brown the brown go gray
- must be the dust
&
the car is covered with rust
must be the sea.

And I glance from my hands to the speedometer
Needle clicking past the years
Blazing through the 30s 40s 50s 60s
dipping into dust; flying into dust clouds
faster!
Now at sixty-three!
Soon to hit sixty-four!
Needle whipping on its way to 65.

Why, there are friends of mine

who never passed eighteen.

Others there were who slammed into trees
at twenty-two -
a few flew into bottles & glasses and shattered
at the thirty mark
& others of my own age had their heads explode
or grew strange brain-blossoms
when they passed the speed of their own sound.

And here am I, leaning on the seat
watching the road, skidding at odd moments
- a lurch - is this it?

A sideways skid/
is this the place
my hands will leave the wheel?

I glance in my rear-view & side-view mirrors
& there they are
friends, a few relatives.

My babies
now with faces of adults
large hands on the big wheel.

On the same road we are driving.

Driving

Driving

Driven.

Ken Lyons.

My father-in-law. Missed by all.
When he was sick and I was on the East Coast with my mother
who was approaching her own death, he'd call me up. Those
calls, simply to ask how I was doing, or to promise me a cold
beer with him when I'd return, still stay with me. He knew I
needed contact, and what I was going through.
I wanted to have this poem ready for what would have been his
80th birthday.

I miss our wide-ranging discussions, and the fun of
remembering Card Games at the Press Clubs on each end of
the country.
This web-address will give you a great sense of a man who
lived life full-out.

http://www.legacy.com/obituaries/theprovince/obitua
ry.aspx?pid=181588267#sthash.juyFLFwm.dpuf

Kenneth Douglas Lyons April 24, 1937 - September 20, 2016

A Creel for Ken Lyons

1:

The weaving of a creel for Ken Lyons
requires only memory
&
the presence of a veteran trout
who knows enough to see
that a fly simply landing on the water,
especially with a hook beneath its feathery under-belly
is not a real invitation.
not for
old fish...
not for
old fishermen
such as Ken
or me.

We have to watch the way the circle spreads,
outwards,
&
lights ripple over water.

We all know
that clumsy fishermen catch
only young fish...
&
Ken was never a clumsy
fisherman.

In life as well as
nearing
death
he took the time to size up where he was.

When infection came along
it carried with it a lake
that poured past emergency
beds in hallways,
lifting curtains around
people shouting
crying
falling through
life.

What Ken felt was
the lake, the peace
how the surface looks when the day is mauzy,
bringing fog to sooth trout
&
fishermen.

Ken Lyons allowed a lake
would be a good place
to go,
unpack a creel, and drop the rainbow trout into
a cast metal pan on
blasty boughs.

Smoke brings with it
the faintest hint of moss upon
the angles of fish scales.

At Six Mile Lake
the rainbow trout
are waiting.
At first they nudge the plant-life on the rock,
swarm (as minnows) around each hook.

Fish and Fishermen know how
to watch the circle of each
falling chunk of the planet,
see circles in the river of the air,
watch shapes, reflections
from our lives,
form living compass spins
fold in more turnings,
and we all
explore and swim
in
ascending
spirals.

Circles
always
work.

2:

While taking
family night shift in the after midnight hours,
the lake grew real for Ken and me.

In the corner of the ward the water spills.
He sees the waters rise.

This lake holds time-beams in its eye
and rises through time itself,
to head towards us.

Suddenly a leg swings up
to hit the hospital bed railing
that keeps Ken from
falling to the floor in
the floating boat
we call a hospital.

He looks at me,
until I speak
and say,
"Ken, catch some sleep. I'm here all night."

He rolls his eyes and closes his lids
and ...
...waits till I almost doze off.

Soon as I nod,
Ken blinks open one eye to check and see if I'm asleep
yet,
and closes it fast.
He has that patience of the deeply ill,
of the real fisherman
who can outlast that night.

One eye stays slightly open, making
sure I stay awake for the full waiting shift
until mist burns off the lake
and polishes the golf course
&
time jumps
&
we all gather
With Pat & Caren & Cori & Darren
to wish him well.

Roll back the years, past
the farewell as
the golf ball flies Happy Gilmore-style
&
travels decades
to bounce and roll
on manicured earth, towards
a hole-in-one
the way a roulette ball will roll
to join just the right number

with just the right gambler.

Roll back the years
in the sky.

Clouds filled with roiling images:
A boy with hair that resembles
Alan Ladd, looking at the camera
as if it contains a horse-race.

A deeper cloud
holds that moment when
Ken and Pat looked across a room
and knew
at once
what we know now
informed by all the years of Pat & Ken
of them laughing with
Ron and with Betty;
the days when being young seemed as easy as
staying on a Carousel.

Roll back the years
before smoke rises
from the lakeshore fire.
&
dust falls back through dust,
into Heraclitean water.

How fast does time go by?

Look...
three boys with fish
held up to brag to camera.

Look...
the camera clicks
and they're back in school.

Look...
One minute he's here,
smiling at the camera,
baseball-cap turned round;
he's casual, smile saying
"It's so great to be outdoors"
away from the Royal Columbian.

Ken pauses for the camera.
Time whirls
like planets.
Time is spun
fast as a flame-spinner
could spin
the hours and the decades.

3:

His smile stays in all our minds
when we see that one photo forming;

a family gathering just a year ago.

O, I remember the day, the shot,
for, what's eternal is memory itself;
even when it goes,
 it remains
beneath
the surface of the lake.

Must have been a
time-spinner that caught
the moments of *here* and *there*
of *now* and *then*
until we all meet at a lake.

A snapshot,
stays in out minds
just a great day on the back deck
and I see wife and family
watching Ken
&
they click mind-cameras
at the exact moment
the
button of the smartphone
is pressed.

Memories never die.

Even when all who were there
have gone, they keep swimming in clear waters of
a lake that lasts forever.

Fish, and fire, and wind, and rain
all float in time.
Memories form again in clouds,
dying and birthing galaxies.

One minute, there he is
just out of the hospital
between visits
and the day, I remember
is eternal.

We may walk in and out,
and we all choose to gather,
for we're spokes of the same hub
turning, turning,
thru nite, day
month year
and not yet here.

One minute.

Turns out,
the weaving of a creel
for Ken Lyons
requires only memory

&
all
may travel home,
no fuss,
with a creel
that's filled
(on
moss)
with memories of Ken.

A little note says it all...
"Gone Fishing.

Epilogue

epilogue:

THE PROPER LOVE OF FATHERS & SONS:

A little boy
is lost in a field of snow gray
twined
grass hairs,
the cookie can
I carried
was gray and red
and bound up with a neighbour's string.

In the lost field
the cookie can was the only wheel to carry me
past the snowstorm
spin me
over the drifts
till you,
father,
found me
and, Brownie Hawkeye first,
asked me to wait before
I ran -
until you had snapped me
in your album.

Then, I ran to
your strong
your lifting
arms
later
wet through
sandy hairs
as you lifted me to my
warm bath.

When I was five, we'd quarrelled
and you stood outside in the hall --
a creak of cigarette smoke --
while mother at my
prayer-stained bed,
where I had willed
your death,
was telling me how much
you loved me.

Even when you strode in the room
and stooped,
I couldn't kiss you,
a-tremble in your fear,
the premonition
that this hope,
this all you ever could become,
this tiny once in a gowned arm
this whooping in the night

might fail you as the world had done
might like the others
turn away.

Years have spun years from the world
and my son is in my arms,
and feet a-kick
he dances baby steps across my waist.
His eyes are lit by
dance steps with me.
His eyes hold sparks of your now quiet flame.

I see you in his eyes
and I remember
the too proper love of fathers
and sons
where all the words are hidden
and even when a father waits outside a door
it may not open.

My son is in my arms
and dances.

This tiny once in a gowned arm,
this whooping in the night,
is laughing
as the music plays.

And in the dance
we leap into
your eyes.

After words:

Acknowledgements:

Photo Album - first appeared in The Proper Lover.
Hounslow Press, 1986.

The Five Philosophy Lessons Of Alexander Stuart Gill
`Mechanic`s Institute` Journal. Australia, 2004.

Nan - first appeared as *A Night In The House* – in The
Proper Lover. Hounslow Press, 1986.

The Man Who Wears His Jacket In All Weather – First
appeared in Contemporary Verse Two Vol. 6 No. 3
Spring 1982. Territories Publishing Co. Ltd.

The Long Walker – First appeared as *Remember Ian* - in
Contemporary Verse Two Vol. 6 No. 3 Spring 1982.
Territories Publishing Co. Ltd.

The Proper Love Of Fathers & Sons - first appeared in The
Proper Lover. Hounslow Press, 1986

Thanks to my friends. After all these years, and all these
travels – every moment was worth it, to discover the
nature of true friendship.
May my poems for those I remember help bring them to
mind again

If you use the web-address at the end of this note, you'll find yourself at a free website where I'll be posting new poems and adding postings about people already featured in this book, as well as experimenting with different forms of this sort of poetry.

I'll add extra links as this idea evolves.

https://shinto-poem-field.yolasite.com/

Gull Pond Books :

Novels:
The Terra Nova Quartet:
  Maud's House
  Chips & Gravey
  Midnight At The Mockingbird Motel
  This Is What I Must Remember
"The Newfie Bullet" Trilogy
  My Newfie Bullet
  Poet In A Pontiac
  Dogs Of A Strange Town
Poetry
Ocean Of Childhood
Shinto Poem Field
Moon Tides

Mystery Series:
Panama Kills!
LA Kills (Summer 2017)
Washington Kills! (Fall 2017)

Children's Books:
The Adventures Of Stumpman

Made in the USA
Columbia, SC
15 July 2017